Chat Rooms is an all inclusive literary focused open mic and independent publisher located in Everett, WA. Find us at Lucky Dime every Wednesday.

Est. 2023

POST MORTEM DANCE FEVER
KRIS HALL

© 2023 kris hall

isbn: 979-8-8690-9347-9

cover by tex gresham

interior design by tex gresham

author portrait by araless

author photo by jennifer robin

published by chat rooms in everett, wa

post-mortem dance fever

kris hall

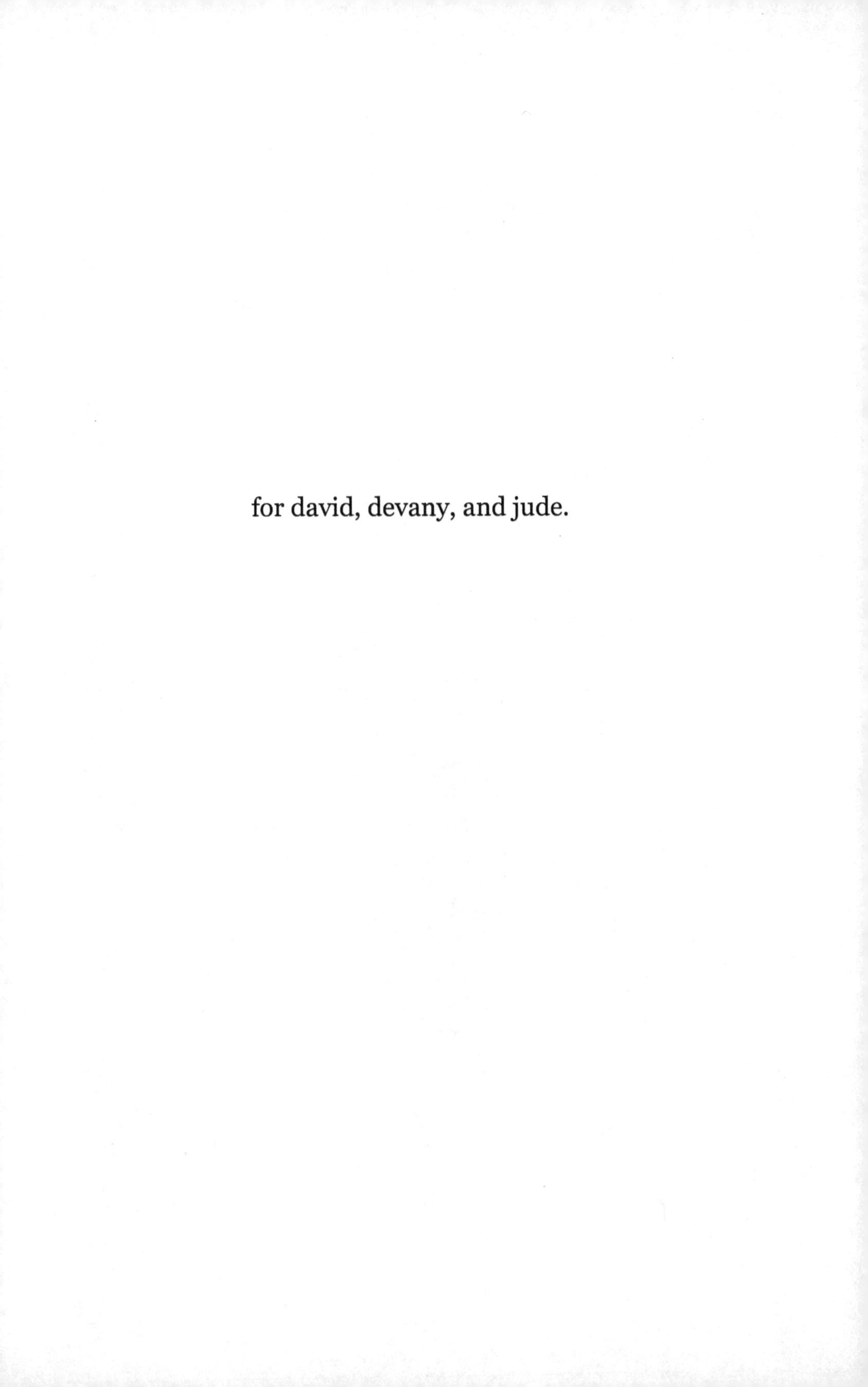

for david, devany, and jude.

one came back and hunted me down,
a wolf like me,
desperate for familiarity

they joked about brandishing
their open-carry
taking me to the beach
& removing my teeth

it was then that i remembered
i can vanish on my own terms

i blame myself, i'm a monster for story
i forget i am vulnerable to its development

it happened again, before
we thought we were like each other

imagine me, shirtless, in my underwear,
sitting in a computer chair in a trap house

fluids lick the eyes

their rituals were different,
left me frozen in my seat

we're not freaks, they said

i know, i replied
i am

in the bathroom stall, without a door,
my piss bubbles look like spider eyes
inquisitive, they analyze my stupid-happy face—
i will not be lunch for the toilet today

in the bipolar mirror, my reflection is obscured
by stickers and sharpie

jokes from the neighboring urinals echo absurdity
to the front of the bar where i head for another

at tony's, where on tuesdays,
i can sink the cue ball for free

where i can see the people i love
on any given day
& the people i don't
aren't ever coming back

(that is not to say i do not miss them
it is to say they are not the people i miss anymore)

reconciling through indifference—
taming spirals
as i pretend to have grown up
without the taste of cola on my lips

some things still yearn to be tasted;
listed safely within parentheticals & blackout

in any direction i turn to blow my smoke,
i can hear the music of the future

outside, where everything is wet with light

a block away,
a giant tears free from its ligatures,

climbs down from a business's rooftop
& points a finger at me
as if to invite me on an adventure,
season to taste new nightcrawlers—
as if to suggest it wasn't already on my mind

pray for the stain on my shirt
the stain from today's chicken teriyaki
the fluttering lonelines in my heart
the way i deal with concerns

pray for the stain on my shirt
wish its origins to shift to love-making
what we've done with the frosting
to spruce free from vanilla

pray for the stain on my shirt
the sign of a stabbing you wish you'd seen
but most likely the way i hari-kiri
myself when i take on olympic banks

pray for the stain on my shirt
that it's only from today
not from yesterday
and that it'll be gone tomorrow

i really like this shirt

it has a picture of a ghost
lifting its sheet up
shining a flashlight up there

it was given to me by a poet
a poet named gib strange

he said, get it,
it's flashing you

      little pervert

stars in the eyes of vampires

vampires with stars in their eyes

tolerating the freaking human

      syntax

their flight is a pulling wind

bloody pizza, blood

is pizza—youth fuel

halloween is over but i'm still thinking about you

like a painted wound

stars in the eyes of vampires

vampires with stars in their eyes

beware! wolf! beware of past midnights

how they stack up

& reveal how low the stakes really are—

no dependents, no familiars

you're going to live forever

as long as you keep telling yourself

you're going to live forever

in the split shine of broken neons
& a half-carrot moon,
gravity is a wirey cage
whenever i bend over,
cue stick in hand,
only to expose my tail,
whipping sharply out the back
of my jeans—

are you haunted enough? i ask

are you haunted enough by the scene
of the razor tip
threatening to cleft
as i miss my bite
on the eight-ball after a sweep?
my win and losses go toe-to-toe;
every streak comes with a scratch

just me, making use of the mundane

it's the repetition that alarms; these episodes
are syndicated reminders of how much work
there is left to be done

no more waiting for the sun
to melt,
to become visible in flames,
a reverse vampire,
burning in the night,
smelling stars explode,
talking my mouth off,
it begins speaking for the ground
pleading to be given height
& a much grander mission
other than to remind me to
pull my pants back up

my cigarette tastes like chicken mcnuggets
unfortunately, i don't think it's one of those strokes

i won't be speaking in new dialects
i won't be painting any hyperrealistic murals

solving complex mathematical equations
i'll just remain fumbling words the way i've always

my cigarette tastes like chicken mcnuggets
& you don't care that it tastes like chicken mcnuggets

this is not something unique to me
i assume none of my experiences are

my cigarette tastes like chicken mcnuggets
there is an urge to dip the little stick into a pack of sweet
& sour

sizzle out and bask in the new fragrance
of burnt condiment

my cigarette tastes like chicken mcnuggets
now i really want chicken mcnuggets

hoping i'm familiar to at least one of these crows
the expression i made at the taste of chicken mcnuggets

i remember what goats look like. this is not one of them. i can't even describe it to you, but i can tell you it is, without a doubt, under the scrutiny of fact, not a goat. however, i have the shrug of an understanding it is a goat. in spite of my truth, it has the exact presence and personality of a goat. it's just not what i remember goats looking like. it is and is not a goat. i remember i was taking a bath when i first saw it (pictures are better with cheese), someone had said being pansexual makes you infallible. the goat showed them its abdominal snowman (a snowman on its abdomen); three tiny apertures of blasted disappearance. all of my wives have cried beside me, it bleated uptempo. as if to say, in goat, it accessorizes with a perforated appendix; crawling on all fours. crying shit like 'evermore, evermore' every morning. edging you for surgery—'evermore, evermore'. on new year's eve i fainted from dehydration and hit my head on the bathroom floor. my genitals exposed as i was pissing when it happened. my friend's curious fingers checked to see if my hair had tangled with the tile and merged. this was not the case; the blood was minimal. i didn't say anything before because i was embarrassed. embarrassed by everything except for when i put it into poetry. on january 1st i admitted myself into the hospital for appendicitis. unrelated to the fainting. unrelated to the goat. my mortality defended once again. as the nurses checked my scalp and back for cuts and abrasions with their soft, curious fingers, i thought of other curious fingers. fingers expecting coarseness only to learn i am soft all over. i will be soft to the touch, for the touch. the goat that is not a goat registers it was only a conduit for cadence in the beginning, hangs its head eeyore, breaks apart into jigsaw pieces in search for tangible connection; a picture as big as the waterfront, framed by the backseat of a car, punctuated by books and cigarettes. soft all over.

i think about what's been on my mind
& inside my body

my cigarette tastes like the weed i put in it
my cigarette tastes like impending unemployment

chocolate sometimes

i think about what's been on my mind
what's put it on its back so many times

fuck for sugar,
fucked for sugar

i'm taking a bath by someone special
i file my fangs down so not to burst any bubbles

though i've been told i've done so in vain
as i appear more shady when i shave

there should be no question that my complications
come invited, as price of admission

this goes both ways;
how to come, acquainted

i think about what's been on my mind
& what it has been telling my body

inseparable, those two
overwhelming, those two

my cigarette tastes like every good
moment with you, weird and spellbinding

i watch you eat plants in public
& you accuse me of seeing you

& i do, with the dilemma being,
i see more than sugar

the antibiotics must be kicking in

headless spray, the neck sprays
the inconvenience of the biological phenomenon;
it happens more often than not

our silences have been recorded, duly noted;
i prefer not to use this information
to meddle in my own life, prepare for grief

you can't ice a sinking stomach,
superglue the virgin feeling;
there were other rules to mention
but they turned up missing

no poets allowed.
poets aren't allowed
to be anything but their star signs & traumas

they wrap themselves in ghosts
write spells, make new friends
they turn into ghosts

something's to be said about a good love poem though
you get to say what you never get to say

'who' is a whoops of creation
the red flowering currant has no name for itself,
for me, before searching
neither would the purged and plunged,
the sense the milieux of barren walls
would make little without context—
sitting in silence,
the other side of our taken breaths
where without you, without you
nothing happens without you

coping through cruelty
with gulash and banana
cream pie, all for practice
for something worse,
because i'm still drawn
to outlaw romances and medussy
—the eventual business
that comes with them—
each finger a different stone

the battuto of anxiety
anneals to no one
preparing for lethologica
when you talk i repeat lethologica
so i don't forget it
lots of intellectual warm ups;
hitting the turf with improper english
and my non dominant hand,
mentally shelled,
choked up by back rubs—
everything about this is falling
off the bone,
fragile though stretchable
i assure to reassure myself
an erasure of our flaws

it's a soft zoo, these energies;
wasted on wondering
if i'm happy, not as happy
as happy but happy
nonetheless

what was david cassidy thinking?
say it three times in the mirror to yourself

before ever putting yourself through that again
i downloaded an audiobook on active listening

but all i can remember them saying is blah,

blah,

blah

not all cold is translucent, just this memory;

gratitude for warm fingers that once
canvassed the vagus

i am a psychic lifeform beholden to likemind
you're screaming at the wall that is my face
my face that looks like a uterus,
armed to the teeth w/ teeth

you've knobbed over to the correct frequency
so i change frequencies to hide the crags
in my thought's voice
but now i'm sharing a channel
with a dreamed spirit, it possesses me

skins me with light

from alien, to another experiment, to exorcism—

now i'm home, eating human food
with indifference
finding it embarrassing
i can only communicate in poem,
billiards, or cribbage;
drink and pizza

what's wrong with small talk and doom scroll
enjoy the common while it is

edited, undone, once the party is

cold open with reverse engineering
the vessel that's become the obstacle—
because you told me so, and
having never been examined,
i am in a constant state of waiting,
waiting in the back rooms
to be researched,
remotely, in my sleep,
a stationary blur,
undisturbed in shrink wrap,
under the magnet of
a violent green—
awake to wooly breath,
some teeth missing, the hairy ones,
scales where the circus animal shaped burns
used to be; biopsies, the taste of
raw root vegetables and dirt,
latex in the air; opening the application
that alerts others of my existence
to find the most unflattering photos
of myself—all pictures i took of myself
i've just been notified i've died
by the worst people—people on the internet
i've just noticed i'm a flickering green glow,
a body of eucalyptus, spritzed
hovering over a pane of crisis which is
no longer my own—
b-sides are records of
what could have been,
more than a two bird symphony,
a host of ideas and magical gestures;
salt of the earth; all kittens and poodles—
the type of person you could rely on
to help you move the lighter boxes
up and down
elevators in secure buildings
looking himself into importance
simply for helping

the other guys are wondering what
he is offering, what he is getting out of
carrying a shoe box of dvds and a flatscreen monitor—
i mean, they're sweating profusely
like towels submerged in a bucket of water
& then wrung out, reminding themselves,
he is helping, he is doing the best that he can

he's kissing honey on the lips
i've got nothing, just a bell
between my legs

seasonal something something
something   i know that it could be enough
some place else

amoebawaty palms gooeystuck,
we're seen as touching through glass

psychic bikinis pit against
the naturally delicious

take it or leave it, you take it
sidled upside beside you

take it or leave it, it takes you w/ mementos,
heartsmacking portraits, bracelets
that weren't meant to symbolize anything

now such accessories tug at you,
intrude with memory and mew
and paw from underneath the door jam
like a cat you've already done everything for
yet it demands further access into your life

your most private and vulnerable positions
what could they possibly imagine is happening?

the tip hasn't hit yet
& i've got enough
for two diet cokes
sure, once it does hit,
it'll put me in overdraft
but, it's fine, i want
two diet cokes
that burn in my throat

not to knock current scripts,
i just question if i'm medicated enough
for a relationship
when my love language
is annoying the shit out of you

the birds are singing
or talking to each other,
i don't really know what they're saying
perhaps commenting on my lived years
people are the same way
the dead at least lend a certain romance
and mystery to the past

though i feel the most like myself
than i have in months,
jordan peterson is still weeping, shoeless,
because i haven't cleaned my room

it's sunday, another day of rest,
i'd rather be with my familiars
practicing my outside english;
a race to eleven, i make it as far as ten,
& if that isn't enough for you
you can sing it to the birds

skeleton flowers
look as edible as fried air
on a bed of cotton candy
whenever you move in
like my last eclipse had

i'll eat the flowers to show you
i'm not crazy

i'll eat the flowers to show you
my credibility

how soft they are against the teeth
you have the trim of the sun
killing just enough, for a moment,
the noise of subjectivity
an appreciation for lost values
illimunes the better parts of the graffiti
you and i smoking all my cigarettes
which never bothers me
because i've made them yours too

a little congregation of laughter
light gossip and truths
some can't bear to stomach

because they've forgotten
how to taste the flowers

which i now know i'd forgotten once, too

mars attacks! makes you laugh
at the fall of troy

indelible warpaint
still paint; still, paint—
differentiation was the purpose
there

i never know what to make of you,
twisted grasshopper,
jiminy snicket, jesus cristobel

        the poets who stalk you

thinking their thinking will deploy love
& if not,

i can't tell you what we're about to see
& how it will influence art

i can tell you, like you,
i'm going to make it about me
to be happy is to be defiant—
show me an aerial view

of walking into limitless rooms
where both the doors and windows
provide passage at the will of
our paper-thin wrists, easy

i woke up today after being awake
for twenty-four hours
on epiphanies,
eating all of the macaroni salad

one of my best familiars is head over heels
& i find that to be so rebellious

it qualifies for awe
in spite of personal history—

i can resist no longer

my heart doesn't sing for you,
that would be stupid
& i'm not finding myself ravenous
things are awkward enough
i just want to help you find your tortoise
& care for this thing
your love transcended dreams for
feed you cold treats &
listen to you recite poetry
as if i'm hearing it for the
first time every time—
you've successfully turned
reading the poem into the
poem, trilling pixie

i heard you whistling in the movie theater
then again at the hospital
i looked for you as i always do
peering over my shoulder to see
if that's you making the laughter happen
by the venue's entrance, my bloodstream
flushed with saccharine cliches
whenever you are found

i cough up rose petals
when you bring me shepherd's pie
i cough up rose petals
when you know of spike fuck
they take flight, inviting complication
your kiss, your love
whatever the price
for admission,
consider it paid

affectionately only
texting your name
to let you know my thoughts
are down bad
beholden
while i wait for a response,
i step out into the ice
smeared lot
enter the presence of corvus
feeding on seeds my neighbors
have thrown from their balconies
i feel comfortable adjacent
to them always
not a mere recognition of existence but
a sense of belonging,
as though these crows today
are the very same murder
i've had witness to my entire life
across all divots and splendors
never given names or acknowledged
beyond a stroll-like stalking,
mesmerized by their animation
& pecking personalities
but today we relate on more than locale
we relate because it's fucking cold out
are you cold?
for now, i have only my hands
to warm you
texting you, affectionately,
only your name, to let you know i see you
among the corvus congregating
just outside my life, tho you're more than
a fun and gothic fixture,
you give my eyes, eyes
an aerial view of the distance worth
to warm you

the shore has grit...

if it only were an easy task to remain verticle
in the face
of the gravity i've instilled

& the tide resisted against raising the ante,
these gams could rest across another pair
without exposing my longing rhythm

the mission is stillness, the mission is to
debrief with a chaotic calm

winning a deck of tarot is not the same
as winning at tarot

at least i know and live by where the water is

i care enough not to do it again
the white sheet over the owl
playfully, a ghost until it
tears through the blindspot in the sky
blinding with uncertainty

where it went

the muskrat makes eye contact with us
knows its fate before we do

makes eye contact the whole time
it's horrific; the eye contact

a beaked vacuum sucking up the hide
insatiable for jeans even

as i fell near fainting on the pebbles,
not far from the fence, i thought
& thought & thought

i care enough not to do it again

you tell me it's everything
about the passion flowers
that you like about the passion flowers
each a flamboyant display
witchy, delicious candy
you go on to tell me how you'd devour
bones & all
these faes surreal and magical
spin to marvel in your belly
& the reaction you give is one
sweet blessing to the receiving end
i wish to create the same response
so i go online and search the earth
for the most adequate deal to
sacrifice my cool lambs with
i imagine the passion flowers marching
through the town
celebrating you with banner and brass
until they inevitably find you at your work,
thawing sausage,
the passion flowers march around you
declare their adoration
triggering a praise kink
that makes you spin three times
squealing levitation
as the surprise is all too much
I give you my hand to reassure you
of your anchorage, as you kick the air
delighted but unsure

feathers, gills, and anime veins in the back of my head
are all i need to display this discomfort

a post-dopamine dump migraine interrupts clarity;
thunderclaps the pleasure into impossible memory

just another side effect of my medication
the price of admission i'll sadly, gladly pay
to remain stable as i spin inside the make-believe—
all natural abilities demagnetized from my body,
as you can probably relate, with your own dr. poison

my posture doesn't help
my eyeglass prescription is outdated, too

but i am stable as a totem top, spinning still
stilling spinning, still going, still living in the privilege of our

times

at the end of an aggressive bender, i woke up to the news
of the inevitable child i'd never have

tiny red arms reaching out through the fire in the caves
whose walls pontificate the reason behind my erasure—i do

not disagree with it

i step off myself like a carousel, i step off on to grounds, tilted,
but familiar

a menagerie of sparks, scintillating horses;
which ways to go to get back on,
which ways to go to get back on,
which ways to go to get back on

i've taken my shirt off
blowing bubbles with death—
its skeleton
& i skinny dip together;
leaping in to the most robust vesicle,
pondering the life-cycles, the color theories
for each of these loose pendulums aplenty

abound above we are bathing in rainbow light
looking at the bubbles below, deep beyond the bottom

death's bony finger points to a reel in a bubble
flashing movie ideas that became movies
made by someone else burdened by motivation

bones point to another bubble containing that sentence

i'd be lying if i said i didn't write it in your voice—
my temporary genius; a big fish

bones trace spherical tomorrow, the debris of our lifestyles
carry over like sand from the beach

not the other sand

sand from the beach

prisms push out shards of poems,
slices of poems,
before they spiritually collide
w/ a wheel made by roads

deflated despite
          everything being a poem

i can't talk on the phone right now

but i'm still present...

nothing beats getting stoned

and thinking you're writing

one of the best poems you've ever written

only to realize the next day

it's just a recipe for cheetos

humbled now, a human with nothing to lose

except for self-respect

the light makes it darker sometimes

comely for this tarot movement —

depending on which art is used

& how it is interpreted, my bag is

either full or overflowing

i walk barefoot on a floor of flamin' hot cheetos

their bag i've emptied

there is a lighthouse on inside the house

an ivory lighthouse shooting ivory knifelight

inside a charcoal shell

the light makes it darker sometimes

say it again, only because you're laughing

       the light makes it darker sometimes

wincing in the view of being seen

mostly by myself when i walk past my blended

reflection in the window of a foxglove

uneasy with a mess for hair,

a missing button and poorly upturned collar

i've seen how sharply i can cut a deck

& will again & again

& it will not involve any poems

it will not involve any prose

when i find a new series to watch,
i'm keeping it to myself—

bombarded by the thought
of all the streaming reality shows
i never finished
because we were done
& they were the only familiars left
to share the laughs with

i'm fickle with entertainment, i'm too
sensitive to the correlating pings
of the lovesick follies,
eyeroll triggered by existence

if i were to keep watching,
i'd expect them to enter a scene,
telepathically gentle & warm on the nose
tripping over power cords and auxiliary cables
whilst eating a toasted bagel, twisted up in the
inconsiderate production of my possible imagination

it was a comfortable city, once
an inglorious phase, on your greener side, i'm sure

it was a comfortable city, once
a place before memory
imbedded the compass

what complaint is this,
under a roof with a bidet
and an electronic toothbrush

the fridge is full and i could keep eating
but nothing sounds good

stacks of books i haven't yet read
rest behind my pillow

i pet the covers and spines with my eyes
to absorb the perfectly bound
intelligence and aesthetics

that may be as far as i'm willing to go tonight
that may be as far as i'm willing to go

not to be a devastated hole
confusing intuition for anxiety
but can you reach inside &
pull at that strand of hair
making everything taste like
the color that it is
distracting from engagement

there's much to catch up on in the group chats
a rash of unread attempts at correspondence
glows in the dark, endless in the oculus of my iniquitous off days

it spreads beyond my person;
               i want these spare limbs to lend a hand
& contribute something, anything, to the discussion
before the neglect becomes contagious

they have proven useful, fulfilling connections
absolutely necessary at times—
i've kept the notifications
as a reminder that the friendships we made
during the war prosper in defiance of
the changing winds

that gods remain armored for similar reasons,
they remember when they were vulnerable,
in magazine cover love with the things
they never got to say, so they could live on as fantasy
rather than embittered memory,
in case it were received in tangles

i want to see you in person, in real life
find each other lost in a department store
lit up like macy's or hallmark,
like it was before the war

i just wanna say, say,
   to your voids, say,
as they are milestones too, i see them, too

   i just wanna say, i'm proud of you—
in my absence, you're doing much better

i put the fire out as quickly as anyone caught on fire would—
i rolled myself up into the rug like a genie brisket,
smothering the immolation

a little weirdo about it, hootin' and howlin'
til i go hoarse;
my victory cigarette tastes as cooked as i do

once extinguished & the double crisp has sloughed
i can play again

that is, if i can remember what i was playing

the triangle must be bermudian—
what did i get in?
am i high ball or low ball?
who racked last?
didn't i just break?
it is a phenomenon that occurs in billiards,
your short-term memory goes kaput
it's hard enough to remember how to outside
english the passage of time
makes a number of faux pas—
we remain ageless here,
both focused and dumbfounded
which would be enough except for
i'm bone dry & starless
& while i'm as tired as the gin blossoms
grew of it
i'm convinced its absence has
defanged me, robbed me of my
post-mortem dance fever
i'm going to ask
if can we play one more game

one more game

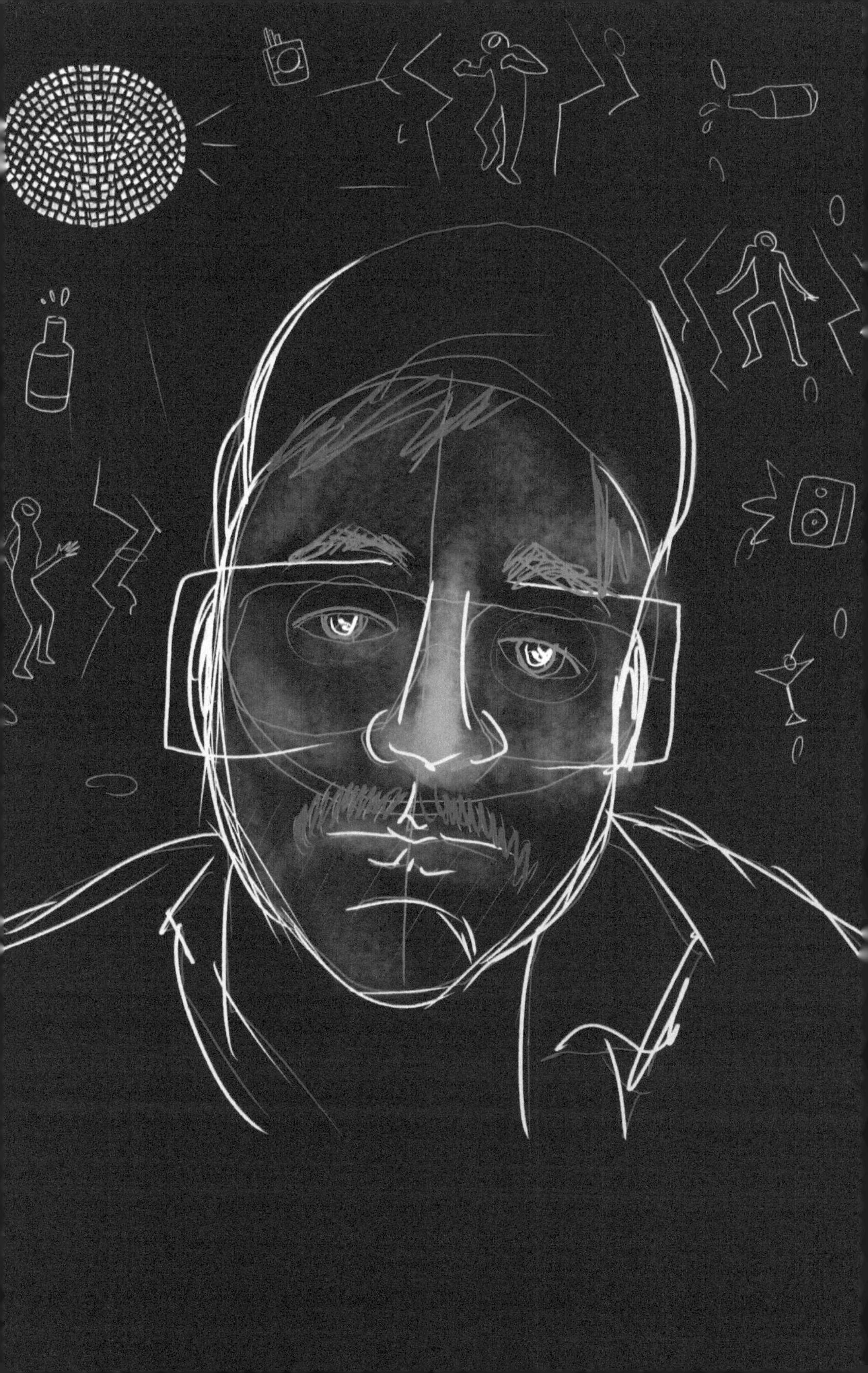

KRIS HALL (aka Barracuda Guarisco; C.C. Hannett) is the author of several collections of poetry and hybrid works published by Spuyten Duyvil Publishing, Vegetarian Alcoholic Press, Really Serious Literature, Feral Dove Books, Voice Lux, Alien Buddha, and Chat Rooms. Widely published in journals, online and in print, they have also been nominated for Best Microfiction and The Elgin Award. They currently reside in Everett, WA.

www.ingramcontent.com/pod-product-compliance
Lightning Source LLC
Chambersburg PA
CBHW061446160726
47995CB00003B/1063